世界宗教博物館
MUSEUM OF WORLD RELIGIONS

Guidebook

Words From The Founder

The Museum of World Religions offers us an opportunity
to learn more about religions,
to choose a spiritual belief for our own life.
It is a place for different religions to freely discourse,
So that there will no longer be religious disputes and conflicts.
This is a museum of the spirit,
The restful and unrestrained destination we seek.

— Dharma Master Hsin Tao,
Founder of the Museum of World Religions

3

A Feast for All the Senses

Welcome to the MWR Guidebook and, indeed, to the museum itself. For those readers who have already visited the Museum of World Religions, may I recommend another, more detailed tour, using this book as your guide to enter the universe, to establish a dialogue with spirituality, and to become familiar with every aspect of the museum.

Ever since deciding on the seemingly insignificant word "museum" almost ten years ago, and despite traveling the world to hold discussions with national and international scholars and visit the best and most varied museums, no one was able to tell us how to combine traditional arts with modern technology. No one thought it possible to present the glory of all the world's major religions in one room, and no one believed it was possible to give concrete expression to the spiritual concepts of love and peace. Most of all, no one seemed to think a nun could get this done. Now, ten years later as this experience comes to fruition, the process, although successful, has been humbling.

Money itself was not sufficient to realize this dream; likewise, having people of talent was, on its own, not enough. What was needed was the spirituality and patience that only religious people possess. Nevertheless, it goes without saying that we were most fortunate to gain the "religious" dedication of everyone involved in this project: Ralph Appelbaum of the RAA museum design company and Prof. Lawrence Sullivan of the CSWR at Harvard, all the monastics and museum staff, and the expert consultants. The museum may not be absolutely perfect, but it certainly derives from absolute goodness.

The designers have created a "Jacob's Elevator" that ascends from the hustle and materialism of street level towards heaven, which leads to the purifying atmosphere of the Pilgrims' Way. Offering a chance to dust off their worldly concerns, this moment of tranquility will enable visitors to better experience

life's spiritual message. This calm grayness gives way to the shining Golden Lobby. Be sure to spend a moment taking in the variety and wonder of the cosmos, its firmament and astronomy, its religion and history, as here are to be found many secrets of space and time.

From outside, the golden lobby resembles an eye of wisdom. Next, the Creations theater resembles life's black box, followed by its opposite, a bright sphere, symbolizing life's consummation. Square and circle, darkness and light, these kinds of intense contrasts are connected together in the Net of Indra, but what is its meaning? Take time to search for answers.

Arriving in the Great Hall of World Religions, the visual displays cannot be described in words. From the feel of the floor beneath your feet to the sounds of each religion, this experience is a feast for all the senses. Moreover, July of 2003 witnessed the launch of the MWR's architectural exhibit, "The Greatest Sacred Buildings", which is located in the Great Hall. Through these skillfully imitated models of important religious architecture, you can further your understanding of a variety of religious symbols and their sacredness.

As you leave the museum taking our blessings out into the world, also leave behind a seed to work with us in promoting life's education.

Dharma Master Liao Yi,
CEO,
Museum of World Religions

Contents

Introduction

By Hung Shu-yen

The MWR is the first museum in Taiwan to take as its theme religions from around the world. On the basis of the religion's antiquity or number of followers, ten major religions were chosen for exhibition, including Buddhism, Daoism, Christianity, Islam, Judaism, Shinto, Hinduism, Sikhism, Indigenous Religions and Ancient Religions. As the MWR is located in Taiwan, naturally it does not overlook Taiwan people's own special beliefs, and these are introduced in a special section entitled Taiwan's Religions.

Most extraordinary is the MWR's use of modern technology and multimedia technology to offer the traditions and cultures of religions the largest possible presentation, while visitors can still gain spiritual stimulation from traditional museum exhibits of religions' beauty.

A tour of the MWR is more like a spiritual baptism. It is not merely a religious exhibition hall, but a living organism, a safe haven in the secular world, and a forum promoting dialogue between religious and spiritual worlds that hopes to reconcile conflict and advance world peace.

The MWR is not only a museum that displays religious artifacts, but it is also a museum for life education. The museum's first director, Pao teh Han, established life education as a primary mission, actively promoting the idea to education centers, while also being responsible for the planning of the religious architecture exhibition, 'The Greatest Sacred Buildings'. He is currently developing an exhibition for children's life education in an effort to extend the concept of building a world religion museum.

The MWR is approximately 7,224 square meters in size, and is located in Yonghe City of Taipei County (above

Sogo Department Store). The main exhibition area occupies the sixth and seventh floors. Seventh floor exhibits include Pilgrims' Way, Golden Lobby, Creations, and the Great Hall of World Religions. These exhibits clearly illustrate the concept of love and peace as the basis for building the museum, and also present different various religions' history, culture, and art in the world through painting, sculpture, ritual artifacts, textiles, and architectural models.

The sixth floor exhibits includes Hall of Life's Journey, Awakenings, Meditation Gallery, and Avatamsaka World. These exhibits use historical artifacts, multimedia, and films to illustrate the value and meaning of birth, coming of age, mid-life, old age, death and afterlife from a variety of religious and cultural perspectives.

This Guidebook to the Museum of World Religions has been produced to allow visitors to continue their experience even after leaving the museum. In simple language and with vivid illustrations, the guidebook introduces the theme, special features and role of each area of the museum, so that readers can understand the essence and glimpse the beauty of the museum. The guidebook follows the path taken by visitors, stopping at each point to give a detailed introduction.

Hopefully, this book will serve as a reference material for both visitors and those readers unable to make a trip to the Museum of World Religions personally.

Floor Plan

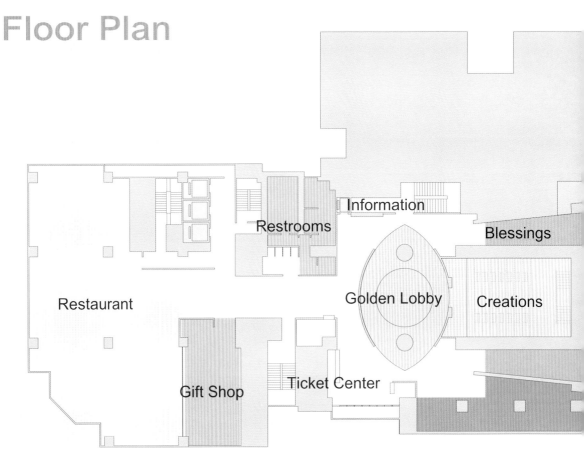

◎7th Floor Plan of the Museum of World Religions

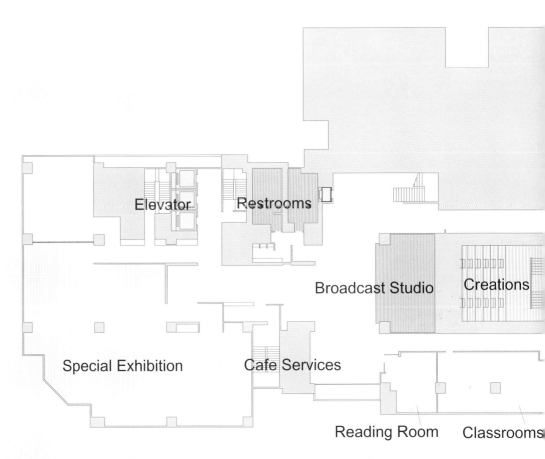

◎6th Floor Plan of the Museum of World Religions

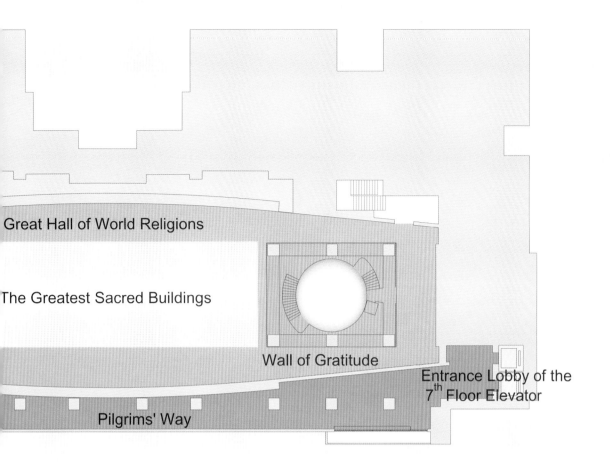

Great Hall of World Religions

The Greatest Sacred Buildings

Wall of Gratitude

Entrance Lobby of the
7th Floor Elevator

Pilgrims' Way

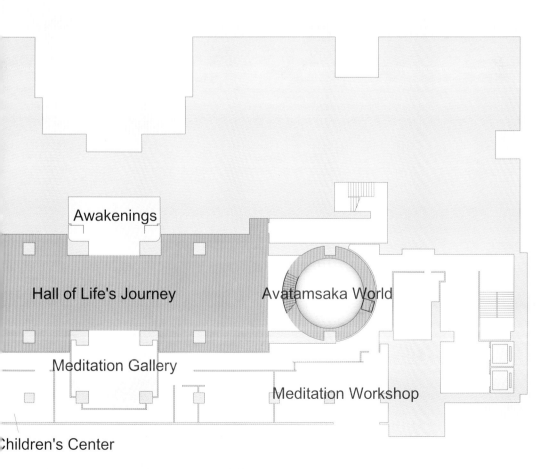

Awakenings

Hall of Life's Journey

Avatamsaka World

Meditation Gallery

Meditation Workshop

Children's Center

A
Journey
in Exploring
Wisdom

真的有神嗎？祂是誰？

7th Floor

Pilgrims' Way

Visitors travel by elevator to the 7th floor accompanied by special audio-visual effects. On entering the Pilgrims' Way, visitors read a quotation concerning enlightenment taken from a gatha (hymn) composed by Master Dao-Hsin, the 4th patriarch of the Chan School of Buddhism, over one thousand years ago:

百千法門、同歸方寸

Expanded in meaning to include peoples of all religions, this is translated as

The doors to goodness, wisdom and compassion are opened by keys of the heart

The Museum of World Religions hopes that this gatha will help visitors understand the wisdom of human life, both ancient and modern, crystallized into the act of pilgrimage. Furthermore, it may offer understanding, nourishment and enlightenment for use in their personal lives and growth, and in dealing with humankind's increasing mutual interdependence. That is to say, the source of all growth and development is to be found within each person's heart.

A purification ritual at the 'water curtain' follows reading and contemplation of the gatha. Water has a special significance for many faiths and is used in ceremonial practices symbolizing the purification of body and mind. Visitors may touch the wall curtain with their hands, representing a cleansing of the heart and spirit, as well as of the hands.

As visitors walk along the gravel surface of the Pilgrims' Way, questions such as "Who am I?" and "Where do I come from?" are broadcast, while images of pilgrims and various religious motifs are projected on the walls. Even before finishing this journey, perhaps visitors may already have found some answers.

On reaching the far end of the Pilgrims' Way, there is a black heat-sensitive wall on which visitors may leave a handprint. Each image represents a visitor's blessing for the Museum of World Religions.

The significance of water for various religions is as follows:

Christianity: Jesus was baptized in the River Jordan.

Sikhism: Guru Nanak, founder of the religion experienced the call of God while bathing in the Bein River in 1499.

Hinduism: Rituals relating to birth, death and everyday activities are purified using water from the Ganges.

Buddhism: The Bodhisattva Avalokitesvara holds a willow branch with which to sprinkle water over people to purify and save them.

Shinto: Visitors to shrines must firstly wash their hands at a font to purify themselves.

Handprint: Hands play an indispensable role in religious ritual. They are used to make gestures, to offer prayers and extend blessings, for healing of giving alms, or for touching the body as a blessing. In some traditions, the hands of god (or gods) created then rule the world, and it is with their hands that humankind reaches out towards their gods and the rest of the world.

7th Floor

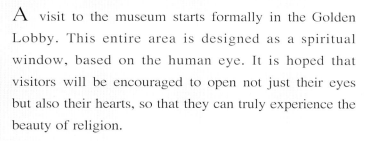

Golden Lobby

A visit to the museum starts formally in the Golden Lobby. This entire area is designed as a spiritual window, based on the human eye. It is hoped that visitors will be encouraged to open not just their eyes but also their hearts, so that they can truly experience the beauty of religion.

Standing in the center of the resplendent golden lobby, visitors can see two great pillars inlaid with gold-colored mosaic on which, in fourteen languages, is written the sentence:

愛是我們共同的真理、和平是我們永恆的渴望

Love is our shared truth - Peace is our eternal hope

This truly represents the founding inspiration of the Museum of World Religions.

For thousands of years people have continually dreamed of the cosmos, developing different interpretations of the stars' meaning that have greatly influenced humanity's worldview. Accordingly, the ceiling of the Golden Lobby represents sacred heaven, and when light from the 12 star signs on the ceiling is projected on the floor, the symbolic bridge between heaven and earth is built.

On the floor of the Golden Lobby is a "Cosmograph" representing the three dimensions of the Cosmos — Heaven, Earth and humankind. It combines traditional images, colors, materials and motifs of the world's various religions. The labyrinthine pattern of the Cosmograph resembles the maze on the floor of the Chartres Cathedral, France, which has been slightly altered to include colors and animal images symbolizing the world's major religions, and adjusted to lie in harmony with the four main compass points on which the MWR lies.

Each color, image and direction in the design has its own religious connotation. In Western traditions, even the process of walking through a maze represents a kind of search for truth. As visitors stand on the design, they may carefully search out each color and image, and work out the meanings they symbolize.

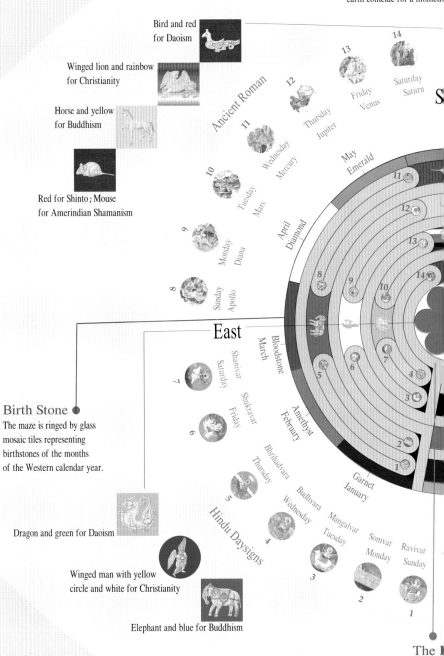

THE GOLDEN LO

In the Golden Lobby, we have comb
from several of the world's religions to create a
of a three-part universe. The ceiling represents t
the floor imply points of entry to the thir
signs of the zodiac in the ceiling strik
earth coincide for a momen

Bird and red
for Daoism

Winged lion and rainbow
for Christianity

Horse and yellow
for Buddhism

Red for Shinto; Mouse
for Amerindian Shamanism

Ancient Roman

13

14

12

Thursday
Jupiter

Friday
Venus

Saturday
Saturn

11

Wednesday
Mercury

May
Emerald

S

10

Tuesday
Mars

April
Diamond

9

Monday
Diana

8

Sunday
Apollo

East

Bloodstone
March

Shanivar
Saturday

7

Shukravar
Friday

6

Amethyst
February

Birth Stone ●

The maze is ringed by glass
mosaic tiles representing
birthstones of the months
of the Western calendar year.

Brihhadvara
Thursday

5

Budhvara
Wednesday

4

Mangalvar
Tuesday

3

Garnet
January

Somvar
Monday

Ravivar
Sunday

Dragon and green for Daoism

Hindu Daysigns

Winged man with yellow
circle and white for Christianity

2

1

Elephant and blue for Buddhism

The

The floo
The maz
This ma
that are

OSMOGRAPH

olors, materials, and patterns
, " - a composite symbolic representation
e floor represents the earth. Windows in
nderworld. When light from the
ones in the floor, heaven and
s to Creations open.

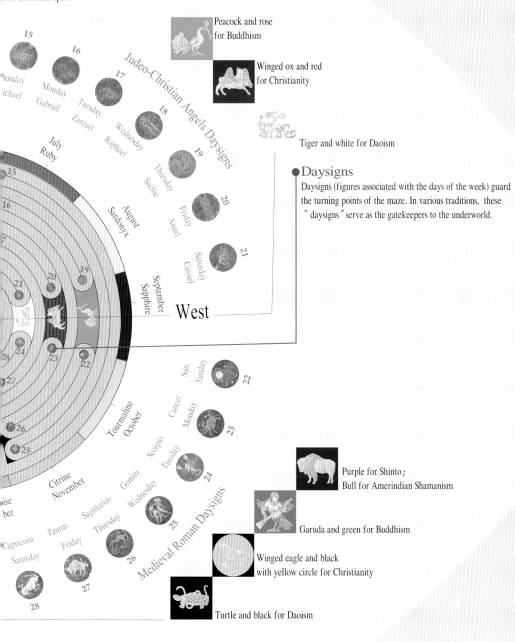

Peacock and rose
for Buddhism

Winged ox and red
for Christianity

Tiger and white for Daoism

Daysigns

Daysigns (figures associated with the days of the week) guard
the turning points of the maze. In various traditions, these
" daysigns " serve as the gatekeepers to the underworld.

West

Purple for Shinto;
Bull for Amerindian Shamanism

Garuda and green for Buddhism

Winged eagle and black
with yellow circle for Christianity

Turtle and black for Daoism

organized in a labyrinth, or maze, derived from one in the Chartres Cathedral.
any traditions, and in Christianity it symbolizes the earth.
dified to include colors and images from different religions
the cardinal points : GNorth, South, East and West.

Creations

With its images and music gathered from the world's religions, and the artistic quality of this theatrical experience, this movie gives visitors a most vivid feeling. A voice over explains ideas about the obscure origins of nature and the impermanent cyclic nature of the universe. This 12-minute film seeks to enlighten viewers' thinking about life, expand their spirituality, and provide a deeper understanding of different religious myths.

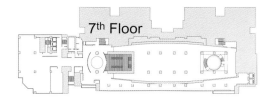

7th Floor

6th Floor

Perceiving the Stages of Life

Hall of Life's Journey

The Hall of Life's Journey is subdivided into five areas: birth, coming of age, mid-life, old age, and death and the afterlife. It examines the interaction between people and religion from the point of human life, birth and growth.

This area makes use of film and multimedia interactive technology, allowing visitors to operate computer screens personally to gain an understanding of various religions' similarities and differences in outlook towards human life, as well as the ways in which religions influence and assist humankind's development. Displays also exhibit artifacts relating to life ceremonies.

Through Hall of Life's Journey, in addition to celebrating good events, visitors can also gain a deeper understanding of religious ceremonies and traditions in life.

Birth

Name: Christian Baptismal Robe
Material: Cotton
Place of Origin: Ireland

Baptism is the sacramental rite that admits a candidate into the Christian Church. The candidate is baptized with holy water, resulting in a "spiritual rebirth", and an expectation that he or she will in the future be responsible for the spreading of the Gospel. When a Christian family decides to baptize a newborn child, they prepare a clean white robe for the infant to wear following the baptismal ceremony. Literally "wearing Jesus Christ" with this robe, the baptized newborn becomes the child of Christ's illuminated light.

Name: Jewish Circumcision Knife
Material: Silver
Place of Origin: Holland

Jewish male circumcision originates from the period of Abraham, who, according to the Hebrew Bible, circumcised himself and all male members of his household in obedience to God's command. Jewish males are circumcised on the 8th day after their birth when they are given a Hebrew

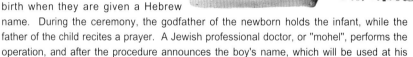

name. During the ceremony, the godfather of the newborn holds the infant, while the father of the child recites a prayer. A Jewish professional doctor, or "mohel", performs the operation, and after the procedure announces the boy's name, which will be used at his future Bar Mitzvah, wedding, and also written on his tombstone.

Name: Christian Baptismal Shell
Material: Silver
Place of Origin: England

The custom of using shells as ritual baptismal implements for newborn children dates back to John the Baptist's baptism of Jesus Christ. The guardian of the child usually presents the baptismal shell as a gift, celebrating the newborn's first contact with Christianity. It is then used to pour water on the child's head during the baptismal ceremony, cleansing or representing the removal of the stain of Original Sin. The back of this particular shell contains the initials of a baptized child, "M.R.S".

Name: Chinese Children's Shoes
Material: Cotton
Place of Origin: China

This traditional Chinese pair of shoes is sewn with patterned images of a tiger. In traditional Chinese folklore the tiger represents vigorous energy, good fortune, and the ability to ward off evil, and this is exemplified in the belief that tiger shoes can protect children from falling when walking. Therefore, Chinese mothers carefully sew images of the tiger onto the shoes for their newborn children, demonstrating the deep love, affection, and hope that they will grow up safely.

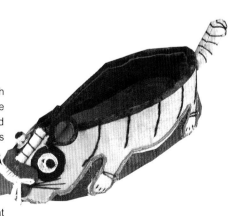

BIRTH

"All men have one entrance into life, and the like going out."

-Holy Bible

初生

「每個人的生命皆有
一個入口，來如出口。」

—聖經

生命是希望的寄託
是命運的存續，
用忠厚的心靈去會託節
感從基地的尾聲中 譜出
無窮的希望，照亮的可能
低迴，死亡革命的聲音
仕事復生命飄起的前途
陶熱 照光

初生　創造　潛在獲致　希望　允諾　生存力
Birth　Creation　Possibility　Hope　Promise　Life Force

成長

COMING OF
AGE

"Fashion your life as a garland of
beautiful deeds."
Buddha

成長 就是人人
感悟無限，慢步成長
成長就是成長
感謝人生旅途成長力量
就在那裡成長
我是我知我行知我
成長那可追成長力量
感謝那成長美麗成長

誕生　　成年禮　　成熟　　人生禮
Initiation　Adulthood　Maturity　Rite of Passage

宗教儀式禮儀　自我發現　自我修正之
Religious Guidance　Self-discovery　Self-definition

Coming of Age

Name: Christian First Communion Attire
Material: Silk and synthetic fiber
Place of Origin: U.S.A.

Christian families consider a child's first communion day to be a great celebration. On this day parents enthusiastically make all the necessary preparations for a child approximately 7 years of age, because at this age it is believed that a child has the ability to understand the meaning of the bread and wine in the Sacrament of the Eucharist, which represents Jesus Christ's body and blood. White communion attire is chosen because it symbolizes pureness, cleanliness, and innocence. Therefore, children not only wear white clothes at their first communion, but also at their baptism and confirmation ceremonies. The white clothes worn at a first communion ceremony include a veil, handbag, and socks, together with a copy of the Bible, invitation card and picture frame. Following the completion of the ceremony, all of these items are to be kept for the duration of child's life.

Name: Jewish Teffilin
Material: Leather and plastic
Place of Origin: Israel

Bar Mitzvah is the ceremony and status of attaining religious adulthood in Judaism, which Jewish males attend at 13 years of age. Following the Bar Mitzvah ceremony, Jewish males are expected to follow all of the Commandments, and are hence called "Son of the Commandment". Teffillin are small scripture boxes that are usually worn by males who have undergone their Bar Mitzvah, and are tied to their foreheads and left arms during morning prayers. Strips of parchment placed inside the boxes are inscribed with extracts from the Torah, which exhort Jews to respect and love God with the whole of their hearts.

Name: Shinto 753 Festival Attire
Material: Cotton and Silk
Place of Origin: Japan

The 753 Festival (Shichi-go-san Festival) is a ceremony held by Japanese parents for their children. On November 15th, an auspicious day in Japan, parents dress their children in traditional Japanese attire and lead them to the neighborhood Shinto Shrine to make a formal visit to the local deity. The purpose of this festival is for parents to submit prayers to the local deity for protection and blessing of their children, so that they may have a happy and healthy life. At the same time, parents present their children with a type of malt sugar, known as "Chitose-ame" (Thousand Year-old candy), representing the hope that their children will have a long life.

Name: Taiwanese Heavenly Contract
Material: Paper
Place of Origin: Tainan, Taiwan

In Taiwanese indigenous religion the Seven-Star Goddess, popularly referred to as "Qi Niang Ma", is regarded as a guardian goddess for children. In a ritual dating back to ancient times, parents lead their children to the Seven-Star Goddess and ask for assistance in their growth and development. When children turn 16 years of age, they return to the temple to repay the goddess for their protection, by giving thanks and offering many luxurious donations. This heavenly contract between the Seven-Star Goddess and the parents enables a child to become the goddess's stepchild, demonstrating the love and hope that parents have toward their children.

Mid-Life

Name: Indian Wedding Attire
Material: Composite materials
Place of Origin: India

In traditional Indian ceremonies, weddings are seen as one of life's important turning points. Through marriage the bride and groom become life partners and are responsible for having a son to carry on the family lineage. A priest, who is an expert in the details and meaning of the ceremony, conducts the wedding and infuses sacredness into the event through a series of rites, including the exchanging of rings and vows. The bride's dress and accessories, such as decorations, make-up, and painted hands and feet, are to be elaborately done and follow traditional specifications. She wears a six-meter long "sari" and two-meter long head veil, made of red gauze with gold embroidery, while gold accessories, such as head-rings, nose-rings, earrings, necklaces, and bracelets, symbolize future prosperity and wealth.

Name: Hindu Holy Rope and Sindoor Box
Material: Cotton, silver
Place of Origin: India

The Holy Rope is a red cotton thread used in traditional Indian weddings. A priest during the ceremony ties the right hands of the bride and groom together with red thread and recites the words of the ceremony, translated as "the connection of hands", symbolizing the eternal connection between the newly married couple.

The Sindor Box holds red powder ground from minerals. The groom during the wedding ceremony puts sindor in the parting of the bride's hair as an expression of love, while praying for a long and auspicious marriage. The color red represents power, and its meaning in Hinduism is derived from ancient sacrificial ceremonies, when blood from sacrificed animals was put on the forehead of the worshipper to bring good luck. Although plant dye or minerals gradually substituted blood in ritual, the meaning of red in Hinduism has still been preserved to this day.

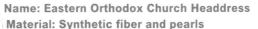

Name: Eastern Orthodox Church Headdress
Material: Synthetic fiber and pearls
Place of Origin: Greece

The wedding crown is an indispensable ceremonial article in Christian Eastern Orthodox traditional weddings. Originally the crown was made from fresh flowers. However, because flowers are difficult to preserve, a headdress made of white pearls has become the common article. In the crowning ceremony of the wedding, two corollas connected by a white ribbon are placed on the altar, followed by a set of prayers. The priest places the corollas on the heads of the bride and groom, which are then exchanged. At the conclusion of the ceremony the priest returns the corollas to the altar. Eastern Orthodoxy believes Jesus Christ and the Church to be unified. Jesus is seen as the "head" or "bridegroom" of the Church, while the Church is looked upon as his bride, just as the husband is seen as the "head" of his wife. Therefore, the crowning ceremony is regarded as the sacred vow of a couple becoming one.

Old Age

Name: Shinto Kanreki Iwaigi
Material: Silk
Place of Origin: Japan

The Kanreki Iwaigi is a traditional garment worn by the Japanese on their 60th birthday. In Japan, at the end of every 60 years is the beginning of a new cycle; therefore, turning 60 symbolizes a new beginning, a return to infancy, and a rebirth. With the family gathered together, the person celebrating his or her birthday dresses in red attire, including an upper garment, called "Chanchanko", and a red headscarf, or "Zukin", because red in Japanese is pronounced "Aka", which is similar to the pronunciation of "Infant"(Aka-Chang). Therefore red apparel represents the rebirth of life and symbolizes the returning to infancy.

Name: Taiwanese Longevity Turtle and Cake Molds
Material: Ceramics
Place of Origin: Taiwan

In Taiwanese popular culture, special pastries are prepared for festivals and at sacrificial offerings for ceremonies such as New Year's, holidays, weddings, and funerals. Patterns on pastries have different meanings depending on the custom and occasion. For the most part, however, these patterns are used as a prayer for luck and congratulations. Cake molds used in making pastries are usually constructed of wood, but ceramic molds are rare. The turtle and peach are traditional symbols of longevity in China, and molds of these animals are designed on special occasions in order to express birthday wishes.

Name: Christian Pyx and Chrismatory
Material: Metal
Place of Origin: Taiwan

Pyx and Chrismatory are religious implements used in the Sacrament of Unction. When a Catholic is ill or close to death and is unable to attend Mass to receive the Sacrament of the Eucharist, a representative of the Church visits his or her home with a Pyx and Chrismatory to minister the sacrament. With the application of sacred oil on the communicant's face and limbs, the grace of God is received, relieving the person's mental and physical pain. The Sacrament of Unction is believed to raise the communicant's spirit, wipe away sin, and escort the believer to heaven safely. Catholics believe that Jesus Christ's body and blood is the source of immortality, and through this people can enter into Heaven.

Name: Tibetan Buddhist Prayer Wheel
Material: composite materials
Place of Origin: Tibet

The Tibetan Buddhist Prayer Wheel is a Buddhist religious instrument, which is constructed in the shape of a tube with a shaft that runs through its center. Placed within the tube is a paper sutra, while inscribed on its exterior is an inscription of the Bodhisattva Avalokiteshvara's heart incantation, or "six syllable" mantra. One cycle of the prayer wheel represents a reading of the sutra inside the wheel, and the incantation of the inscribed mantra, "Om mani pad me hum".

OLD AGE
"I grow old learning many things."
—Solon

「我因年老漸失所有，
將為冬季收回泥土。」
—布萊克

步法已達近起衰敗

新別讓老漸漸的一生

得知生命過程的喜悅

面對將留下我還遠近？

生命生活分析的

一我未擁有轉還彈著

法所將得更好更已見。

智慧、尊重、領導統御、權威
Wisdom, Respect, Leadership, Authority

Death and Afterlife

Name: Eastern Orthodox Church Shroud
Material: Cotton
Place of Origin: Greece

The Eastern Orthodox Church shroud of traditional funerals derives from Jesus Christ's crucifixion. When Jesus was taken down from the cross, his apostles wrapped his body in a clean burial cloth. After 3 days the miracle of Jesus Christ's Resurrection took place. In Eastern Orthodox funerals, shrouds are used for burial. Over time numerous designs of the shroud have developed, however the main topics portrayed on the shroud are prayers from scripture, the Crucifixion, and the miracle of Jesus Christ's Resurrection.

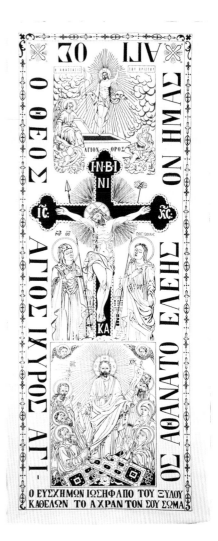

Name: Tibetan Sky Burial Bugle
Material: Animal bones and metal
Place of Origin: Tibet

Sky Burial is the Tibetan custom of cutting a deceased person's body in pieces for vultures to consume. Tibetans believe vultures prefer to eat the remains of the dead with good karma. So when the deceased is believed to have bad karma, a priest uses a bugle to call the vultures to eat the remains of the corpse.

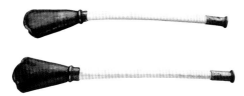

Name: Taiwanese Paper Money
Material: Paper
Place of Origin: Taiwan

Paper money is given to the deceased to use in the netherworld, and can be either burned or placed within the coffin. There are two kinds of paper money: public and private. The backside of private money is printed in the shape of a sawtooth for ghosts to easily grasp. In Taiwanese indigenous religion, it is believed that a person must borrow money from officials in Hell before his or her birth. Therefore following the death of that person, money that was borrowed has to be returned.

Public money is made from rough yellow paper, and one bundle of 30 bills is wrapped in white paper, representing ten thousand dollars. In Taiwanese traditional funerals, there is a ceremony called "surrounding paper money" in which relatives of the deceased in this ceremony surround the paper money hand-in-hand to witness its burning in order to prevent looting from other ghosts.

Name: Egyptian Book of the Dead
Material: Papyrus
Place of Origin: Egypt

The Egyptian Book of the Dead is a scroll of prayers and incantations. The size and the content in each section of the book vary according to the amount of the scroll purchased. Book of the Dead can be placed next to the deceased or painted on the coffin or walls of the tomb. It was believed that Book of the Dead could help a person pass through the dangers of the underworld to Heaven safely. This work was painted by a modern Egyptian artist, and shows the jackal-headed god Anubis, adjusting the scales on which the heart of the deceased is being weighed against right and truth, symbolized by the feather, while the ibis-headed Thoth stands ready to write down the verdict. Recorded in the painting is the oath of the decease's pure and innocent heart with his requests for a fair judgment.

死亡及死後

DEATH &
AFTERLIFE

Awakenings

Using recorded voices and pictures, the Awakenings theater brings together the sacred moments, experiences and life testimonies of world religious leaders, important figures and everyday people. Captured on film, they talk about transforming events in their own lives that led to spiritual awakenings and new directions.

It is hoped that this material will find a resonance in each person in the audience irrespective of his or her stage and status in life, and inspire positive change.

Over humankind's long history, personal contact with god (or gods) and unique tales regarding the power of prayer long ago became an established tradition within many religions. Visitors can listen to people from around the world and learn about their unique perspectives and experiences of life and religion. Perhaps these will correspond to feelings and experiences of their own, create a deeper awareness of life, and lead to a personal awakening.

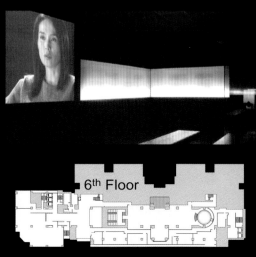

6th Floor

Meditation Gallery

The Meditation Gallery has three large screens, on which are broadcast details of the contemplation and meditation methods used by Buddhists, Daoists, Christians, Hindus, Muslims and Jews. In addition to watching the films, visitors may deepen their understanding by reading the introductory texts and explanations provided on the panels to either side.

The English word "meditation" is derived from the Latin word "Meditari", meaning deep and single-minded thinking. As a religious practice, meditation can be divided crudely into two main types, active and passive. The former affirms the qualities, strengths or moral values of an individual's existence. The latter emphasizes a complete renunciation and transcendence of existential thought. The meditation process should begin with an initial stage of purification and harmonization. The meditator should then seek renunciation and transcendence of ego, leading to personal transformation. Finally, this realization should be integrated into everyday life. In this way, meditation can help a person become more compassionate in their relationship with the rest of the world.

6th Floor

6th Floor

Avatamsaka World

The design concept for this space comes from the Avatamsaka Sutra: One is all and all is one. It expresses the idea that there is wisdom and character common to all religion and all life. This area appears as a glittering sphere suspended in mid-air. By absorbing the visual and audio sensations visitors grasp the spirit of Avatamsaka World.

The film played in Avatamsaka World is projected on a dome-shaped ceiling, containing reflections of humanity's shared history. It is hoped that through this film visitors can share their sacred and mysterious experiences of the Cosmos and enter into the spirit of Avatamsaka World.

聖母升天堂

Discerning the Beauty of Religions and Art

Great Hall of World Religions

There are two main displays in the Great Hall of World Religions: one is the Religions of the World , and the other is the Greatest Sacred Buildings.

Religions of the World

The ten major religions in the Great Hall of World Religions were chosen on the basis of history and number of followers. Eight of these, including Buddhism, Daoism, Christianity, Islam, Hinduism, Sikhism, Judaism and Shinto, are given permanent display, while the other two, Ancient Religions (Egyptian) and Indigenous Religions (Maya), have special rotating exhibitions. In addition, there is a specific section devoted to Taiwanese Popular Religion.

The names and symbolic motifs of each religion are engraved into the floor of the Great Hall to represent the theme of each section. Through artifact and multimedia displays, visitors can gain an understanding of each religion's tradition, history, development, rituals, organization and festivals. Televisions displaying images and sounds connected with each religion further assist in portraying the beauty and diversity of each religion. These finally combine to symbolize the features shared by all religions, love and peace.

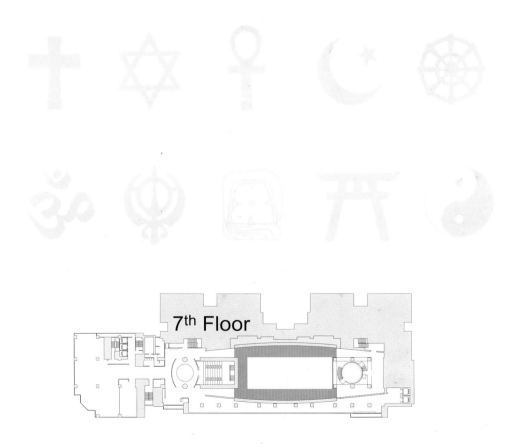

7th Floor

Buddhism

Stele of Buddhist Trinity
Material: Limestone
Time Period : 542 CE
Size : 36.2 x 15.1 x 73.5 cm

This statue was made in the 8th year of the Datong reign of the Wei dynasty (542 C.E.). It depicts the Buddha in the "Voluminous Clothes Great Sash" style, sitting cross-legged, his hands adopting the dama mudra (vow-making gesture) and abhaya mudra (fearless gesture). His halo contains eleven small Buddhas, while to either side are the bodhisattvas Manjusri and Vimalakirti above lions. The back bears an inscription and image of the donor, explaining that a Buddhist named Zhao Jing and his family made the statue, and that the Emperor and commoners alike might gain peace and happiness.

Buddhapadas (Buddha's Footprints)
Material : Grey Schist
Time Period : 2nd century
Size : 45.7 x 45.5 x 8cm

In early-period Indian Buddhism, Buddha was represented by his footprints or some other distinguishing feature. Praying to these footprints was considered akin to praying to the living Buddha, and believed to remove negative hindrances.

Relief Sculpture of Buddha's Birth
Material : Green Shale
Time Period : 3rd century
Size : 50 x 56.5 x 12 cm

Depicting one of the many stories concerning the Buddha's life, this statue shows him being born from the side of his mother. As was customary for pregnant women, Lady Maya was returning to her family home and had stopped for a rest in Lumbini Deer Park. Holding a branch of the "tree of no worries," the Sakyamnui Buddha emerges from her right torso and is received by an attendant, while other maidservants stand to either side.

Islam

Page of Large Qur'an
Material : Parchment
Time Period : 9th-10th Century
Size : 28.7 x 38.2 cm.

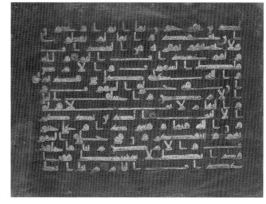

The Qur'an is the fundamental scripture of Islam. Learning the Qur'an by-heart or making copies of it are benevolent acts by which Muslims display reverence for the scripture. Although hand-copied editions exist in many languages, most use the Arabic language in which the word of Allah was announced, and which later developed distinctive calligraphic arts.

This page comes from the so-called Blue Qur'an, a rare Kufic manuscript of the 9th or 10th century, written in gold ink on blue-dyed parchment. It covers verses 187-194 of the 3rd Sura. The relatively few words of elongated script with resplendent decoration, and the uniformity of fifteen lines to a page show that execution of the whole text followed meticulous rules. This luxurious Qur'an displays veneration for the scripture and suggests its patron was a wealthy and powerful aristocrat.

Brass Basin
Material : Brass
Time Period : 14th century
Size : 45.3 x 15.5 x 4.3 cm.

The Islamic world is famed for the quality of its craftsmen's skills and their contribution to the development of metalware technology, in particular the manufacture of brass and bronze articles for everyday use, often inlaid with gold and silver, or engraved with texts.

This brass basin, dating from around the 14th century, was used to contain fresh water or foodstuffs. It is engraved in ornamental script with a blessing and prayer.

Kiswa from the Ka'ba
Material: Cotton and Silk

All well-bodied Muslims are expected to make the hajj pilgrimage to Mecca at least once during their lifetime. The Ka'ba, a square-shaped stone temple in Mecca, is Islam's holiest site. Some 2 million people make the hajj each year. Since the 9th century, the Ka'ba has been covered with a cloth known as the kiswa, on which are hand-embroidered Islamic sayings and qur'anic texts. It is changed each year, when the old kiswa is taken down, cut into short lengths, and given to organizations connected with Islam. This section of kiswa, a sacred object of incomparable value, was given to the museum by the World Muslim League. On it, in gold thread, is embroidered the 82nd verse of the 20th sura: "But, without doubt, I am He that forgives again and again, to those who repent, believe, and do right, who, in fine, are on true guidance."

Egypt

Statuette of Bastet
Material : Bronze
Time Period: 664-332 BCE

The goddess Bastet became very popular in later periods. She has a woman's body with tight-fitting clothing and a cat's head. Small statues of Bastet were placed in temples and worshiped for good health.

Statue of Horus
Material : Bronze
Time Period: 664-332 BCE

Appearing as a falcon, the god Horus represented the pharaohs. This statue wears a crown, symbolizing the unification of Upper and Lower Egypt. Statuettes of Horus were placed in temples for use in devotional offerings.

Judaism

Megillah (Ester Scroll)
Material : Wood; Parchment
Time period: 18th century
Size: 17.4 x 164.7 cm.

This book in the Torah records how the Persian queen, Esther, confounded Haman's scheme to exterminate the Jewish people. Jews commemorate Esther at Purim, reading her story with great clamor, shouting out and stamping their feet each time Haman's name is mentioned.

Shiviti (Synagogue Plaque)
Material : Brass
Time Period: 19th century
Size: 28.2 x 45.3 x 0.8 cm.

A shiviti is a votive tablet placed in the synagogue and faced by worshipers during prayers. It symbolizes that God is looking at them. On it are embossed the Ark of the Covenant, the Ten Commandments, and the word "east" in Hebrew, indicating the direction to the holy city of Jerusalem.

Sefer Torah
Material : Wood and Parchment
Time Period: 19th century
Size: 58.7 x 2423.5 x 11.1 cm

The Sefer Torah is a scroll that contains the Pentateuch, the five books attributed to Moses found at the beginning of the Torah, the most sacred Jewish text. This scroll is written on parchment from right to left and wound around two spindles to form the azei hayyim, or "tree of life". During worship in the synagogue, the Torah is raised and recited, then stored within a covering cloth or a case, and placed inside the Ark of the Covenant in the synagogue.

Christianity

Saint Peter
Material : Oil Painting
Time Period: 17th century
Size: 50 x 63.8 x 1.5 cm
Saint Peter, who was originally called Simon, was the foremost among Jesus' twelve disciples. After Jesus' death, Peter assumed responsibility for the church in Jerusalem, becoming early Christianity's first leader. He is considered by Catholics to be first in a continuing linage of popes.

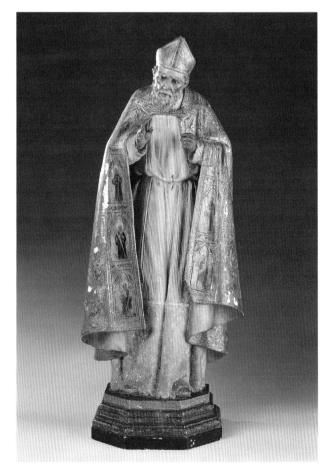

Saint Nicholas
Material : Wood and Gypsum
Time Period: 18th century
Size: 26.4 x 61.5 x 19 cm
According to tradition, St. Nicholas was a 4th century Bishop in Asia Minor. He later became known as the patron saint of Russia, sailors and children, and more commonly, Santa Claus.

Ciborium
Material : Copper
Time Period: 19th century
Size: 17.7 x 54.5 x 18.1 cm

This Ciborium takes the shape of an Eastern Orthodox Church, with the front doors allowing access to the paten and chalice. The other three sides of the Ciborium depict stories from the life of Jesus in copper relief.

Taiwanese Religion

Supreme Emperor of the Dark Heaven
Material : Wood
Time Period: Awaiting Verification
Size: 57 x 96.8 x 52.4 cm.

Anthropomorphic representation of the "Dark Warrior." Representing the northern direction, he is shown without hat or shoes, standing on a turtle and snake, his ancient symbols. He is also worshiped as the founder of butchery and the protector of sailors.

Seventh Lord and Eighth Lord
Material : Wood
Time Period: 20th century
Size: 18 x 37.8 x 14.1 cm. (Seventh Lord)
　　　15.4 x 49.5 x 14.5 cm. (Eighth Lord)

The Seventh Lord, originally known as General Xie Bi-an, is nicknamed "Lanky Lord." in Taiwan. He is recognizable by his tall hat bearing the words "Good Luck on First Sight", the fan he holds in his right hand, and his long tongue, which hangs from his mouth. Together with the Eighth Lord, he helps Cheng Huang Ye (the City God) arrest evil spirits.

The Eighth Lord, originally General Fan Wu-jiu, is nicknamed "Little Lord", and works to subdue demons and monsters. His small hat bears the words "Great Wealth on First Sight"; his eyes are large and staring; he holds a fire tablet in his left hand and a chain in his right hand.

Tu-di Gong (Lord of the Land) Shrine
Material: Sandstone
Time Period: Awaiting Verification
Size: 16.5 x 20 x 12.7 cm. (statue)
　　　101 x 77 x 137.5 cm. (shrine)

Such shrines are made of stone or brick resembling miniature temples. Inside stands a statue of Tu-di Gong, "Lord of the Land". An ancient, simple form of worship is made to this deity in farm fields and every part of a village or city.

Hinduism

Relief of Vishnu
Material : Granite
Time Period: 9th century
Size: 48 x 161.5 x 7.3 cm

Vishnu is one of the three main Hindu deities. As Preserver of the Universe, he safeguards the world. He holds various objects symbolic of this role, including a conch, which symbolizes the origin of life; a dharma wheel, which represents the cyclic nature of time and the seasons; and a mace, the symbol of knowledge and power of the mind.

Surya (Sun Deity)
Material : Black Schist
Time Period: 11th century
Size: 44.5 x 78X19 cm

Hinduism has various sun deities, including Surya, records of whom appear in the Vedas (1500-500 BCE). Each of Surya's hands holds a lotus flower, while in front of his lotus petal throne there is a charioteer controlling seven horses. To either side are his attendants Pinggala and Dandi, while above their heads the wild animals symbolize Surya's universal realm. Above his head is a pair of flying Asparas, with a small attendant behind each of them.

Flute-playing Krishna (Incarnation of Visnu)
Material : Bronze
Time Period: 16th Century
Size: 15 x 29.5 x 11.8 cm

Krishna is the eighth incarnation of Vishnu. In the human realm, he appears as a enchanting cowherd, and is one of the most revered deities in India. This statue of Krishna has four arms; the left rear hand holds a shell, the right a chakra wheel representing Vishnu; the front hands play a flute (lost), showing the charm of the shepherd.

Steel Bracelet (one of Five Ks)
Material : Metal
Time Period: 20th century
Size: 7.6 x 0.79 cm

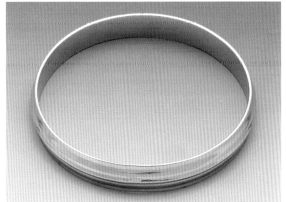

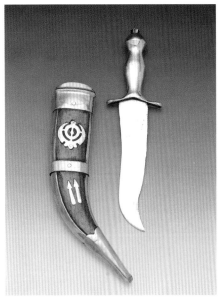

Dagger (one of Five Ks)
Material : Metal
Time Period: 20th century
Size: 6.5 x 27.7 x 2.15 cm

Comb (one of Five Ks)
Material : Wood
Time Period: 20th century
Size: 35 x 5.55 x 0.9 cm

In 1699, Guru Gobind Singh founded the Khalsa (community of Sikhs), and asked all Sikhs to wear five symbols: uncut hair (kesh), comb (kangha), dagger (kirpan), bracelet (kara) and undergarment (kachh). As all begin with the sound "k" in Panjabi, they are known as the "Five Ks." Wearing the Five Ks is a sign of allegiance to the Sikh community, and a reminder to follow the example of the guru's actions. Short breeches symbolize moral fortitude; the dagger symbolizes determination to defend the truth; the bangle symbolizes loyalty to god and the gurus and union with the community; the comb shows a concern for appearance and restraint of desires.

Adi Granth Seat
Material : Wood with Tinfoil
Time Period: 20th century
Size: 96.8 x 157.5 x 59.4 cm.

This kind of seat is a throne on which the Sikh scripture, the Adi Granth, is placed. It is ornately decorated and furnished with cushions and a golden cover embroidered with the Khanda, the symbol of the Khalsa (Sikh community). As an incarnation of the gurus, it is treated with the same respect as one of the ten human gurus.

Maya

Maya Altar
Material : Pine
Time Period: 21ˢᵗ century
Size: 120 x 95 x 75 cm

This is an elaborate representation of an altar from the Chiapas highlands of Mexico. Altars function as the centerpiece of public and domestic ritual activity, often adorned with both indigenous and Christian themes. They are pivotal for the Day of the Dead celebration, providing a sacred space where offerings are placed.

Hanging Textile
Material : Cotton
Time Period: 21ˢᵗ century
Size: 40.5 x 72 x 0.1 cm

This hanging textile piece shows the distinct weaving style of San Andres, a Tzotzil Maya community in Chiapas, Mexico. This handmade piece displays the brilliant colors and intricate designs that make these weavings some of the finest in all of the Chiapas highlands.

Shinto

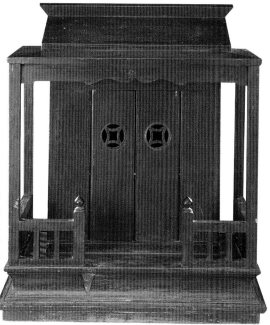

Kamidana ("God-Shelf")
Material: Wood
Time Period: 20th century
Size : 48.8x42x30.8 cm
Kamidana ("God-Shelf") are domestic altars on which people make offerings to gods. They resemble scaled-down Shinto shrines, and are generally dedicated to local tutelary gods or the deities of Ise Grand Shrine. Every morning and evening, offerings including salt, rice, and water are placed on Kamidana.

Shishi-Komainu (Lion-Dogs)
Material: Stone
Time Period: 1185-1333 C.E.
Size: 29.5x48.5x43 cm
26.1x49x44.8 cm
Also known as "Korai" (Korean) Lion-Dogs, the lion with its mouth open and haku (lion-dog) with mouth closed, form a pair in front of the main temple of the shrine. Defending the shrine by preventing danger or evil spirits from entering, they are an indispensable architectural feature of Shinto temples. Most are made from stone; others of wood, iron, bronze, or ceramic.

Sanno (Mountain King)
Material : Painted Wood
Time Period: Early Muromachi era (1338-1476 CE)
Size:13.1 x 35 x 8.8 cm. (left)
14.5 x 37.3 x 9 cm (right)
Almost every mountain and hill in Japan has its own deity worshiped by local people. These are generally known by the title Sanno (Mountain King). This pair represents two of the Hiei-Zan; to the left is Daigyouji-no-kami; to the right is Yamasueno-oonushino-kami.

Daoism

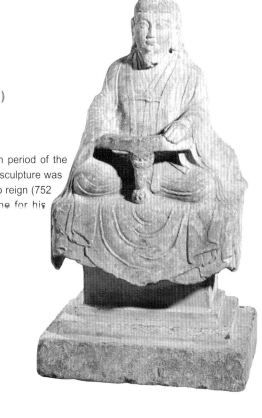

Chang Yang Celestial Venerable (Laozi)
Material : Stone
Time Period : 8th century
Size : 37.5 x 81.2 x 24 cm.
Stone-carved sculptures surviving from the Kaiyuan period of the Tang dynasty are very rare. The inscription on this sculpture was made by Mao Chu-ke in the 11th year of the Tianbao reign (752 C.E.) as an act of merit to beseech good fortune for his deceased daughter in the afterlife.

Illustration of the Daoist Pantheon.
Material : Paper
Time Period : Awaiting Verification
Size : 148.5 x 67.8 cm. (painting)
     220 x 82 cm. (frame)
Deities of the Daoist pantheon are arranged vertically on this hanging scroll. At the top are the Three Pure Ones; below, are a great range of deities including, down the center, Dong Wang Gong (Eastern Prince), Queen Mother of the West and Dou Lao (Mother of the Great Wagon). Such scrolls are generally used for ceremonies.

Queen Mother of the West
Material : Wood
Time Period : Awaiting Verification
Size : 59 x 33.5 x 102.5 cm.
Known by various names, Queen Mother of the West was adopted by Daoists from ancient beliefs and promoted to become part of their pantheon of deities, where she is the most revered female goddess.

The Greatest Sacred Buildings

The displays of the Greatest Sacred Buildings were first exhibited in 2003, and chosen for their unique historical value and architectural features. All of the architecture models on display are constructed either thirty or fifty times smaller in scale than the actual structures they imitate. Of special interest are manually operated mini and microscopic cameras, which viewers can use to peer into the buildings' sophisticated interior, their paintings, sculptures, and architectural structures. Through this process people can experience the architecture's unique visual presentation and actually put themselves into the world of these sacred buildings.

7th Floor

Dome of the Rock

Religion: Islam
Period of construction: 7th century C.E.
Location: Jerusalem, Israel

Dome of the Rock was built in seventh century C.E. by Caliph Abd al-Malik of the Umayyad Empire, and is located on Mount Mariah, in the Old City of Eastern Jerusalem. It is listed along with the two most important mosques of Mecca and Medina as one of the three most celebrated mosques in the world. Building of Dome of the Rock started between 685-688 C.E., and according to temple records, was completed in 692. Judaism, Christianity, and Islam all venerate the site on which the mosque is built, because it is believed to hold the "sacred stone" on which Abraham prepared his beloved son Isaac as a sacrifice to God, and from which Mohammed is said to have ascended to heaven.

Throughout its long history Dome of the Rock has undergone many building modifications, but the overall structure of the mosque has remained intact. Shaped in the form of an octagon, each side of the mosque measures twenty-one meters. Gold foil covers its glimmering dome, which is clearly seen from every part of the city, while the dome's apex holds a crescent moon motif. Exterior walls are made of marble with mosaic patterns inlaid in Arabic style decoration, while the upper sections of the walls are adorned with script from the Koran.

The interior of Dome of the Rock consists of a circular corridor that surrounds the central sacred stone. Four stone pillars and twelve masts support the weight of the mosque's twenty-four arches that bear religious inscriptions of two hundred and forty meters. Since it is considered idolatry to worship God in human or animal form, furnishings are de-emphasized, with the mosque containing neither statues nor portraits. On the other hand, upper sections of the interior walls are inlaid with ornamental decoration, and indicate a highly sophisticated artistic style that must have taken generations to develop.

Luce Chapel

Religion: Christianity
Period of Construction: 20th century C.E.
Location: Taichung, Taiwan

Luce Chapel, which is situated in Tunghai University Campus, was built as a memorial to Dr. Henry W. Luce (1847-1941), who had devoted his life to preaching and higher education in China. Construction of Luce Chapel was finished in 1963, under the sponsorship of Henry R. Luce, eldest son of Henry W. Luce, while American Chinese architect I.M. Pei designed the building, in cooperation with the first chairman of Tunghai University Architecture Department, C.K Chen.

Luce Chapel is a landmark and symbol of Tunghai University, successfully uniting religious atmosphere with architecture. The chapel was designed not only to reflect Chinese cultural traditions and reveal the spirit of Christian love, but also to create an architecture that reflected a modern outlook. The original design of the chapel was based on gothic style architecture, but was cancelled after considerations of earthquakes in Taiwan. After thoroughly researching the project, it was decided to design Luce Chapel with four curved surfaces, or "parabolic hyperboloids", that were to be built separately onto the Chapel. Two curved surfaces to the rear of the chapel were built over the altar at a greater height to partially overlap the two curved surfaces at the front, providing the altar area with more interior space. Separating curved surfaces made it possible for a "skylight" to be created on the backbone of the building, making use of natural light to illuminate the interior.

Although it was originally considered a disadvantage in the project, Tunghai University Architecture Department Chairman C.K. Chen made the decision to construct Luce Chapel facing east. This design allowed sunlight to shine through the windows and illuminate the golden cross of the altar located in the western end of the building, helping worshippers attending morning services heighten their mystical experience.

The four curved surfaces of Luce Chapel are covered with waterproof diamond shaped glazed bricks. These glazed bricks in combination with fillisters built into the bottom of the surfaces help to emphasize the curved design of the exterior, as well as provide wonderful contrast to the checkered design of the interior.

Golden Temple

Religion: Sikhism
Period of construction: 16th to 17th century C.E.
Location: Amritsar, India

The Golden temple is located in the northern Punjab city of Amritsar, and stands erect in the middle of the Eternal Lake, or "Pool of Nectar". The fourth guru Guru Ram Das (1543-1581) excavated the sacred lake that surrounds the temple, while the fifth guru Guru Arjan (1563-1606) completed construction of the Golden Temple's main structure. After construction in 1604, the sacred Guru Granth Sahib (Adi Granth) was moved to the Golden Temple for community worship. Today the temple serves as an important symbol of Sikhism, sacred pilgrimage site, and important political and religious center.

The architecture of the Golden Temple conforms closely to Sikh tradition. The main body of the Golden Temple consists of a rectangular three-story building, with the main shrine located on the first floor. Five domes in the shape of an inverted lotus blossom sit atop the building. The temple's upper half and its interior rooms are adorned with gold foil and verses from holy scripture, while its lower half is made of pure white marble with carvings of auspicious animals. Open to the public at all times are entrances to the building on each of its four sides, expressing the idea that the temple is equally open to everyone, irrespective of race, nationality, caste, or gender.

The sole entrance to the shrine room of the Golden Temple is an archway, while a causeway connects the temple to the patrikrama (pathway), which surrounds the sacred lake. More than sixty meters in length and constructed of marble, the causeway is usually crowded with disciples of Sikhism and tourists, particularly when the holy Guru Granth Sahib is being carried into the shrine room.

Directly facing the entrance to the Golden Temple is the Akal Takht, a three story-fortress-style building. First built by the sixth guru Guru Hargobind (1595-1644) in 1609, the Akal Takht is now an important religious and political center for Sikhs. Apart from the room where the Guru Granth Sahib is kept at night, there are also display platforms where weapons used in the past by Sikhs are exhibited.

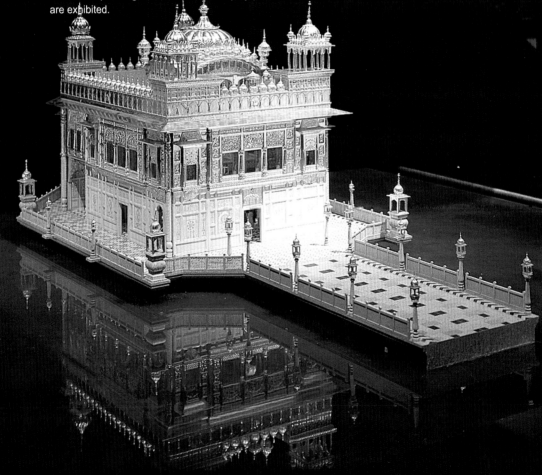

Ise Grand Shrine

Religion: Shinto
Period of Construction: 2th century C.E.
Location: Mie Prefecture, Japan

Ise Grand Shrine holds the most honored position of all shrines throughout Japan, and is considered the spiritual home of Japan's national government and society, housing the sacred mirror (Yata no Kagami) of the Sun Goddess Amaterasu, one of the three items of Imperial Regalia legitimizing the emperor's authority. Situated within a large forest region in Southern Honshu, Ise Grand Shrine annually attracts over seven million people who travel there to make a formal visit.

The two most important buildings in Ise Grand Shrine are the inner shrine, or Naigu, which is dedicated to the Sun Goddess Kami Amaterasu, and Geku, the outer shrine, dedicated to Toyouke No Omikami, the ancient goddess of farming, food and harvest. In "Shikinen Sengu", an over one thousand year old traditional ceremony that occurs every twenty years, the shrines are dismantled and replaced with identical structures on an adjacent plot. Naigu and Geku therefore appear to have been recently built, "untouched" by time.

Ise Grand Shrine's architecture is derived from the style of ancient storehouses and granaries, and is of utmost simplicity. Set within two fenced rectangular compounds, the inner and outer shrines are constructed of plain Japanese cypress wood, which is left unpainted and unvarnished. Floors stand approximately seven feet above pebble-covered ground supported by stout poles, and roofs are covered with long brown reed thatch. These roofs are topped with gold, following the ancient "divine brightness", or shinmeii style, while distinctive X-shaped end rafters, or chigi, together with a series of cigar shaped logs, or katsuogi, lie at right and acute angles to the roof's ridge. The numbers of katsuogi used for shrines vary, with some shrines containing even numbers of katsuogi and others containing odd numbers. Even numbered katsuogi are said to enshrine female goddesses, while odd numbered katsuogi enshrine male gods.

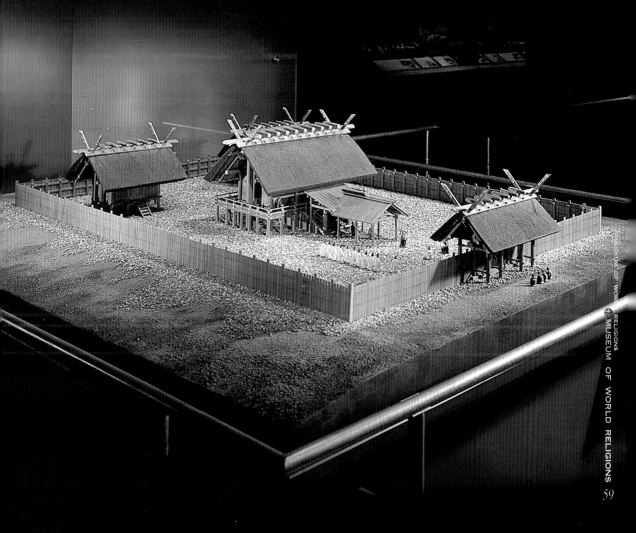

Kandariya Mahadev Temple

Religion: Hinduism
Period of Construction: 10th to 11th century C.E.
Location: Khajuraho, India

Situated in the western section of the Khajuraho Temple Complex is Kandariya Mahadeva Temple. This temple is dedicated to the Hindu god Shiva, with its name consisting of the words, "Kandariya", or cave, and "Mahadeva", another name by which Shiva is known.

Kandariya Mahadeva is the most evolved and representative architecture in India's Chandela Dynasty period of the tenth and eleventh centuries. Structurally, the temple rests on a large base platform four meters in height and is massive in scale, with its lofty curving tower soaring thirty-five meters from the ground. Numerous interlocking steeples and vertical clusters of carved figures contribute to the temple's indented plan, helping to create a visual rhythm that is carried up into the elevation of the building, melding at the top of the temple. The interior of Kandariya Mahadeva, on the other hand, is quite simple. The temple combines three sanctuaries, including a small shrine dedicated to Shiva, a shrine dedicated to Shiva's wife, Parvati, and a central sanctuary that houses a large lingam statue, phallic emblem of Shiva. Surrounding this inner sanctum are connecting corridors with side and front porches. Since the temple's balconies and entrances receive little natural light, the inner sanctuary is poorly illuminated, creating an almost cavelike atmosphere that contrasts wonderfully with the exterior of the temple.

The sheer number of temple carvings at Kandariya Mahadeva is overwhelming. Carvings on the outside of the temple include a large assortment of male gods and female goddesses. Their expressions are serene, majestic, and lifelike, with some of the most important objects of these carvings showing their subjects in alluring postures, while wall relief depicts the ecstatic atmosphere of the gods' heaven, with beautiful flying celestials, and amorous couples shown in erotic embraces, reflecting the creative way in which eroticism is seen in Hinduism, as one of the infinite number of ways to express love for the deity.

Chartres Cathedral

Religion: Christianity
Period of Construction: 12ᵗʰ to 13ᵗʰ century C.E.
Location: Chartres, France

The history of the Christian Church is one of sacrifice, struggle, victory, and triumph. Churches of early Christian history were small and modest, with emphasis on interior church decoration. However, the growth in power and prestige of the Church gave way to more intricate and elaborate building designs that sought to present the Kingdom of God on Earth. This is especially the case from the twelfth and thirteenth centuries, with Christianity's most important development in architecture-the Gothic Cathedral.

Chartres Cathedral is located in the city of Chartres, northern France, on the banks of the Eure River. The Cathedral was built from 1145 to 1170 C.E., but after a devastating fire, the main structure of the current cathedral, with its characteristic two distinct bell towers of differing size and dimensions, was built from 1194 to 1260.

As with most Gothic architecture, Chartres Cathedral contains slender stone pillars in combination with narrow ribs of pointed arches that help support the building's cross vaults. Stone columns connected to exterior walls, known as flying buttresses, were also added to support the weight's main thrust. These features enabled architects to build churches of greater height, create more room for sculpture, and develop larger window designs.

The interior of Chartres Cathedral is designed in the shape of a traditional Latin cross. The middle section of the floor contains a labyrinth design, while the eastern side of the cathedral connects to Aspe Chapel, or Parte absidle, which houses relics of the saints.

The main entrance to the West facade consists of three arched doorways, or portals. These portals contain several lifelike figure carvings of thin bodies with serene expressions, and with fluent, gracefully flowing robes. The right portal contains a carving depicting the birth of the Christ Child, the left portal depicts Christ's Ascension into Heaven, and the central portal contains a carving of the Resurrection. On the North facade of the church, the sculptures of the tympanum present the theme of, "the coronation of the Virgin", while carvings of the South facade portals praise Jesus Christ, His disciples, martyrs, saints, and angels, together with demons, and beasts.

Buddha's Light Temple

Religion: Buddhism
Period of Construction: 9th Century C.E.
Location: Shanxi Province, China

Buddha's Light Temple is located on Buddha's Light Mountain, twenty-five kilometers northeast of Wu Tai county, Shan Xi province. The temple was founded in the reign of the Norhern Wei Xiao Wen Emperor (471～499C.E.) and faces west, with an open and clear view of the area, while mountains surround the three remaining sides of the building. The entire temple complex is divided into three courtyards, and their foundations are all built on the mountainside in terraced field style. In all, there are more than one hundred and twenty buildings within the temple complex. However, Buddha's Light Temple is the most important of these, because it is one of the largest wood architectural structures of the Tang Dynasty (618-907 C.E.)

The main hall, or "Great Eastern Hall" of Buddha's Light Temple is situated on the highest courtyard, majestic in appearance. This hall is the most important building of the complex and oldest surviving representative model of large-scale Tang Dynasty wood construction. The front and back of the building each measure thirty-four meters, while the sides are approximately eighteen meters. Important structural features of the main hall include its pillared wooden framework and brackets that support the roof's crossbeam; complex architectural elements that have their own independent function, yet are tightly intergraded into the building's overall architecture.

Displayed along the main hall's walls are murals of five hundred arhats together with two hundred and ninety-six arhat statues, which both date back to the Ming Dynasty (1644-1911 C.E.). Thirty-five gigantic clay Buddhist statues of the Tang Dynasty pained in vibrant colors dominate the hall's central area. Thirty-three of these statues are of important Buddhist figures, including Sakyamuni, Maitreya, Amitabha, Samantabhadra, Manjusri, Attendant Bodhisattva (who appears to the side of Buddha statues), and Jin-Gang-Dhyana. The remaining two statues are of the temple abbot and sponsor who supported construction of the temple. Combining architecture, statues, calligraphy, and painting, the main hall unifies Tang dynasty art and demonstrates the value and importance of Buddha's Light Temple.

Borobudur

Religion: Buddhism
Period of Construction: 9th Century C.E.
Location: Java, Indonesia

Located in Indonesia's Java region is the massive Buddhist monument Borobudur, which literally means, "stupa on the hill". Although construction dates back to 9th century C.E., the monument was buried deeply under volcanic ash and not discovered until 1814 by English colonist Sir Thomas Stamford Raffles.

In Borobudur's excavation, archeologists discovered color stains of blue, red, green, black, as well as bits of gold foil, and concluded that the monument that we see today — a dark gray mass of stone, lacking in color-was probably coated with white plaster and painted with bright colors, serving perhaps as a "beacon" of Buddhism.

Structurally, Borobudur is a stone monument built in the shape of a steeped pyramid. It contains ten levels that are divided into three sections: lower section, or hidden foot, main body, or rectangular terrace, and top level, known as circular terrace. The sides of Borobudur measure one hundred and twenty-three meters, and contain sets of central staircases that reach the top of the forty-two meter high monument. The lower and main body levels of the monument are constructed in the shape of squares while the upper levels consist of a series of concentric terraces. These levels decrease in size as they rise to a central stupa, peak of the monument. Winding corridors surround the main body's five square levels, and atop the balustrades, each set into its own niche, are Buddha statues, while the upper terraces on the top three levels contain seventy-two hollow stupas, each housing an image of a seated Buddha gazing outward. Since the upper terraces are circular in design, they help give the appearance of a pyramid when viewed from the side, while an overhead view of the monument presents an image of a three-dimensional mandala. Therefore, Borobudur's architecture incorporates three of the most important symbols found in Indian design: the holy mountain or pyramid, the mandala, and the stupa.

Assumption Cathedral
(Trinity St. Sergius Monestary)

Religion: Christianity
Period of Construction: 15th to 18th century C.E.
Location: Zagorsk, Russia

Trinity St. Sergius Monastery is located in the small town of Sergiev Posad, on the outskirts of Moscow. This monastery was built between the fifteenth and eighteenth centuries of the Common Era, and is of great historical importance to religious architecture in Russia, because it serves as a memorial for Saint Sergius of Radonez (1322-1392 C.E), founder of the monastery in 1337, and leader in Russia's fight against Mongol dominance. In the aftermath of Russia's victory over the Mongols, Saint Sergius was given the title "Saint Russia", while Trinity Monastery became the spiritual symbol of protection for the country.

Trinity Monastery began to flourish in the fifteenth century, not only as a community church, but also as a military fortress. In the mid sixteenth century, Czar Ivan the IV celebrated the destruction of Mongolian power, unification of Russia, and expansion of Russian territory by honoring eight Russian saints with the reconstruction of eight main churches, including Trinity Monastery. Four lofty walls and twelve military towers were built to surround the original monastery, while Assumption Cathedral, which is located within the monastery complex, was constructed in imitation of Kremlin Assumption Church.

Assumption Cathedral is the largest and most remarkably striking church in Trinity Monastery. Construction of the cathedral started in 1559, and took twenty-seven years to complete. Four blue domes and one gold dome, all of onion shape, sit atop the Cathedral's pure white limestone walls, combining to create a uniquely resplendent church architecture.

Donations from successive Czars helped Assumption Cathedral acquired the grandness in construction that it has today. With exception to its rich collection of books and historical materials, this cathedral holds two of many famous religious artifacts: one of them is a door decorated with the work of the famous icon painter Andrei Rublev, the other being the Mitre Czar Elizabeth Petrovena gave to the Patriarch in 1744. Therefore, due to the importance of Assumption Cathedral, in 1993, in its seventeenth meeting, UNESCO drafted a resolution naming Trinity St. Sergius Monastery as World Heritage Site number 657.

Altneuschl (Old-New Synagogue)

Religion: Judaism
Period of Construction: 13th century C.E.
Location: Prague, Czech Republic

The synagogue originated from the period of the Babylonian exile in 586 B.C.E. with the Babylonian Empire's capture of Jerusalem and destruction of the Temple of Solomon. Jews exiled to Babylon created meeting places for the Sabbath where they could participate in scripture reading, recitation of psalms, and almsgiving. The Roman Empire's destruction of the second temple of Jerusalem in 70 C.E. marked the beginning of a "Second Diaspora", lasting for almost two thousand years. Over this period, traditional ceremonies of the temple began to be practiced in the synagogue, elevating the buildings' importance. Thus the synagogue became a symbol of Judaism, reminding the Jewish community of its history, tradition, and culture.

Located in the old Jewish quarter of Prague is Old-New Synagogue, or Altneuschl, oldest surviving synagogue in Europe. The original name of the building was "New Synagogue". However, it was not until the sixteenth century when other synagogues were established in Prague, that the building became known as "Old-New Synagogue". Opinions vary concerning the age of the building, but the general consensus is that Old-New Synagogue was built between the eleventh and fourteenth centuries. Richly adorned with stonework, this synagogue displays several aspects of the architecture of the middle ages, containing stained glass windows, a gable, octagonal columns with leaf shaped decoration, vaults, and gothic style pendant lamps.

A small hall and an added southern vestibule for the use of men constitute Old-New Synagogue's main hall, while rooms to the northern and western sides of the building are reserved for women. Furnishings in Old-New Synagogue are modest and without statues or portraits. The center of the synagogue holds a wooden ark that symbolizes the Ark the Covenant; it faces Jerusalem and contains the Torah. Hung over the altar is the Star of David, symbol of Judaism, while encircling the ark are a series of small offices, classrooms, and meeting rooms.

Old-New Synagogue is a testament to the desire of Jews to hold on to their heritage. Despite the many catastrophes that this synagogue has withstood, it still remains active, holding services and housing in conjunction with Prague Jewish Museum one of the finest collections of Jewish art in the world.

Wall of Gratitude

Over the ten-year course of its founding, the Museum of World Religions has received generous encouragement and support from groups and individuals around the world. In order to express thanks to these people, the museum has specially designed and built a wall of gratitude, on which the names and handprints of these supporters are engraved. Interviews with these sponsors who tell the story behind their donations are also broadcast on the wall.

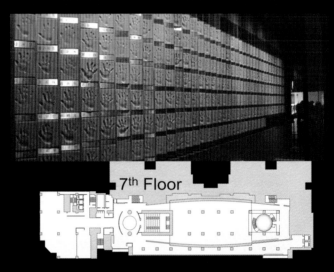

7th Floor

Blessings

Before finishing their visit to the Museum of World Religions, visitors pass through the Blessings Area, where they may touch two engraved handprints on the wall, producing a blessing projected on the screen. Visitors may take this blessing with them as they set off once more on life's journey.

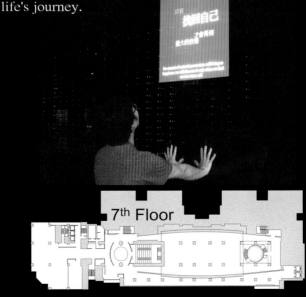

7th Floor

Other Services

6th Floor

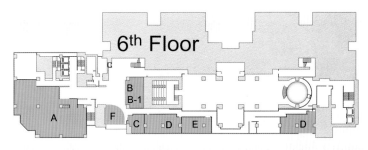

Special Exhibitions (6F)

This space for special exhibitions features material borrowed from other museums in Taiwan and abroad, special themes, and activities. It is also a display area in which religious artists and writers from Taiwan and around the world can exhibit their work.

Broadcast Studio (6F)

There are several multi-media computers set up in the Broadcast studio. Visitors may use the information technologies available to choose from a variety of religious films and music. The opening hour is same with museum's.

Computer Games Room for Children (6F)

Computer games concerned with subjects of life education are offered in this room. Children can learn respect for life through fun and entertaining games. The opening hour is same with museum's.

Reading Room (6F)

Visitors can browse freely through a large collection of religious, artistic, and educational books and magazines. The opening hour is same with museum's.

Classrooms (6F)

People wishing to hold educational activities can rent this space. Contact number: (02) 8231-6699 ext 103

Children's Center (6F)

This space is designed for children's educational programs. Activities are held occasionally to help children develop their imagination and other abilities through games, art, and film.

Muse Cafe (6F)

Coffee, teas, and Chinese and Western meals are offered.
Opening Hours:
Tuesday to Sunday:10.00 -19.00 Closed on Mondays.

7th Floor

H G

Restaurant (7F)

Lien-Xin Yuan Vegetarian Restaurant (7F): Simple vegetarian food, hot and cold drinks, fruit, Chinese and Western meals are available in the Lien-Xin Yuan Vegetarian Restaurant.
Opening Hours: Daily 11.00-21.00.

Gift Shop (7F)

On sale are replicas of artifacts in the museum's collections, sacred objects representative of each religion, as well as publications, bookmarks, jewelry, watches, CDs, calendars, T-shirts and so forth. Representing the essence and best each religion offers, they make excellent gifts or souvenirs of a visit to the Museum of World Religions. Opening hours:
Tuesday to Sunday : 10.30-19.30 Closed on Mondays.

Location and Directions to the Museum

By Public Bus
1. Lines 706, 297, 275 (auxiliary), or 51: Get off at Paosheng Road Intersection.
2. Line 243: Get off at Ren Ai Park, walk south to Paosheng Road Intersection and turn left, then walk for about ten minutes.

By Subway (MRT)
Take the Nan Shi Jiao Line to Ding Xi Station, and leave the station by Exit 2. Then:
1. Transfer to any bus lines 706, 297, 51, Orange 6, or 243
2. Transfer to the "Free Bus for Younghe residents-Line A" (from Dingxi Station), or "Free Bus for Yonghe residents-Line C" (from Yong An Station)
3. Walk to the museum (it takes about 15-20 minutes).

Suggested areas for Parking
1. Ren Ai Park Public Parking Lot
2. Underground Parking Garage of Sogo Department Store

Museum Hours
Tuesday to Sunday: 10.00 - 17.00   Closed on Mondays

Address
7th floor, 236 Zhong Shan Road, Section 1, Yonghe, Taipei County, Taiwan. R.O.C
Tel：（02）8231-6699 Fax：（02）8231-5966
Website: http://www.mwr.org.tw

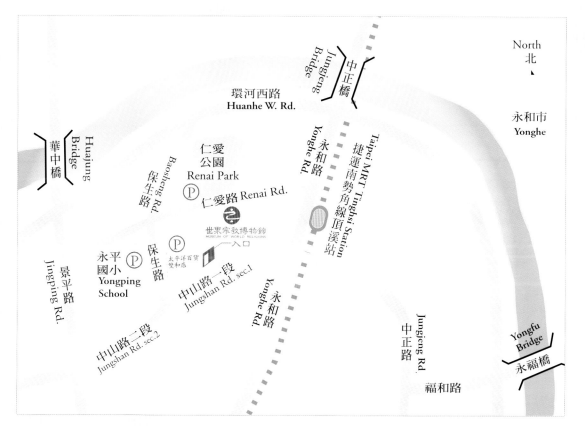

Appendix

Chronology of Dharma Master's interfaith event:

1989	1990	1991	1992	1993	1994	1995	1996	1997

Announcing the plan to establish a Museum of World Religions.

Founding the Center of Buddhist Studies.

Registering the Museum of World Religions Foundation. Participating World conference on Religion and Peace in North Africa.

Visiting Middle East and Turkey. Attending Asian Conference on Religion and Peace in Thailand.

Setting up the Preparation Office of the Museum of World Religions.

Visiting temples and museums in Japan and Korea.

Cardinal Francis Arinze of the Vatican visits Dharma Master Hsin Tao.

Visiting Russia and meeting with different religious leaders of Orthodox, Shamanism, and Tibetan Buddhism. Visiting the United States, and South Africa.

Participating the Sacred Land Project organized by Archbishop of Canterbury, United Kingdom.

When our minds are at peace, the world will be at peace.

~ **Dharma Master Hsin Tao**

All religions teach us to make this world a better place. Yet, religions often are an excuse for conflicts. To build a consensus of co-existence and mutual understanding among the various religious communities is a crucial task.

A decade in development, the Museum of World Religions is dedicated to exploring the diversity of the world's great religious traditions and their interconnections. The museum reflects the vision of Dharma Master Hsin Tao, the founder of the museum and the spiritual leader of the Ling Jiou Mountain Monastery. He conceived the museum as an educational institution that would encourage greater religious and cultural understanding.

Dharma Master Hsin Tao gives his life efforts to foster dialogues among people of many diverse faiths and backgrounds, and provides global outreach initiatives to extend the vital messages of tolerance and peace to a worldwide audience. As he always says: there is only one earth, and we are all one family.

Pope John Paul II awards a benediction to recognize Dharma Master Hsin Tao's efforts on religious dialogue.

Working together with UNESCO to host an extended Buddhist and Muslim Dialogue on" Global Ethics and Good Governance" in UNESCO/Paris. Participating various peace and academic conferences in India, Thailand and Spain.

Attending the meeting of Council for a Parliament of World's Religions as one of the main speakers, along with His Holiness Dalai Lama and Nelson Mandela, Former President of South Africa.

Organizing a series of Buddhist and Muslim Dialogue to strengthen the friendship between religions. The dialogue series took place in Columbia University/New York, Kuala Lumpur/Malaysia, and Jakarta /Indonesia. Founding an International peace NGO "Global Family for Love and Peace" to facilitate peace activities, and later, participating the United Nation's NGO meeting.

Participating the Millennium World Peace Summit at United Nations.

Opening of the Museum of World Religions on November 9th 2001. More than 200 religious leaders from thirty-eight countries attended the ceremony. Announcing 119 as "World Religions Harmony Day ".

Name	 世界宗教博物館 MUSEUM OF WORLD RELIGIONS Guidebook（English Version）/ Second
Publisher	Shih Liao Yi
Editor in Chief	Hung Shu-yen
Text	Hung Shu-yen
Description of Artifacts	Museum of World Religions, Exhibition Dept.
Photography	Ag Chen / Zheng jin-ming
Proofreading	Hong Chih Shih / Katia Ho / Alicia Davis /Emily Chou / Yi-Chun Liu Shu-Yun Ho / Pei-Pei Ma / Jian-Jun Wang / Hung Shu-yen
English Translation	Matthew Lenehan
Art Design	Jacky Mu
Publishing Company	An-long Color Printing&Reproduction Inc.
Post Office Account	18871894
Account Name	Museum of World Religions Foundation, Publications Dept.
Price	150 NT dollars
Address	7th floor, 236 Zhong Shan Road, Section 1, Yonghe, Taipei County, Taiwan. R.O.C
Telephone	(02) 8231-6699
Fax	(02) 8231-5668
ISBN	957-29564-0-X
	Date of Second Publication : April 2004

Library of Congress Cataloging-in-Publication Data